Dried Flower Style

Dried Flower Style

Cameron Shaw

WEIDENFELD & NICOLSON

LONDON

Text © Cameron Shaw, 1997
Photographs © Weidenfeld & Nicolson, 1997

Russell Longmuir has asserted his moral right to be identified as the author of this book in accordance with the Copyright, Design and Patents Act 1988.

First published in Great Britain 1997
by George Weidenfeld & Nicolson Ltd
The Orion Publishing Group
5 Upper St Martin's Lane
London WC2H 9EA

A CIP record for this book is available from the British Library.

ISBN 0 297 83210 7

Designed by Lisa Tai
Edited by Tessa Clark
Photographs by Phil Starling
Typeset in Bembo

Printed and bound in Italy

Contents

Introduction

✳

I always find it difficult to answer the question 'What do you do for a living?'. If I say that I arrange dried flowers, people invariably think of the old-fashioned pieces that were popular with their grandmothers or that they see in pubs. If I say I am a designer or sculptor, this can conjure up different images. I hope this book will change all that.

My introduction to dried flowers was through my sister who already had a lot of experience in arranging fresh and dried ones and was setting up her own company. I joined her originally to organize the business and handle sales and accounts. We began working from our dining-room at home and, as we became busier, I became more hands-on and learnt the basics of how to arrange flowers. Then, as I met more clients to discuss their requirements, I found I was able to offer them fresh ideas for pieces that had never before been created. All I had to do was to turn these concepts into reality.

At first, as I learnt the different textures and capabilities of each flower, it was very much trial and error. The same is true today. It is five or so years since I began creating floral arrangements and I still have a head full of ideas waiting to be tried. In this book I hope to break down some of the barriers and myths that surround flower arranging and show how simple it can be to create a piece that some would regard as a masterpiece.

-1-
Getting Started

*

This chapter takes you through the basics of arranging flowers: how they are dried, and how to choose both the flowers and the foliage; the equipment you will need; and the different types of containers you can use. It also has another purpose: to inspire you to create your own, truly amazing arrangements and floral sculptures.

Drying Techniques

✳

Most people are aware of the basic flower-drying processes. Everyone has seen pictures of Victorian country kitchens with bunches of flowers hung to dry above invitingly warm Agas. They are still hung upside-down today, but in a warm, dark, airing cupboard instead.

I am not going to dwell on home-drying as it has been written about so often and because now, more than ever, the dried flowers, fruit and vegetables available in shops are of a supremely high standard, competitively priced and easily available. A few years ago there were only a few varieties, and dried flowers were seen as a poor substitute for fresh ones – people were afraid to experiment with them. There was very little variation in colour, and none of the vividness that is now so abundant. Today it is possible to buy anything from artichokes and chilli peppers to fruits and hollyhocks. The vast majority of flowers are grown and dried in Holland. They are harvested and then sent to the dryers, often in pre-arranged bunches, as specific orders will have been placed earlier in the year. If they are being air-dried they are placed on mobile racks which are put into temperature-controlled cells. Everything has a different drying time – wheat, for example, dries overnight, whereas artichokes can take up to three weeks – and their position in the cells is determined by this. The artichokes, for example, are placed at the back and remain there until they are dry. Flowers with shorter drying times are moved

Dried roses are ever-popular.

around at the front. This slow and gradual process is used to prevent browning. Freeze-drying is a relatively new and expensive method – flowers are literally frozen in special machines – and produces dried specimens that are identical to fresh ones. This method is very useful for fruit and more open-stemmed varieties like lilies and daffodils. Another technique is to place the flower heads in silica and cover them with it. This removes all the moisture and the flowers are preserved. The latest method is to bleach the flower head and then re-inject it with a special preservative and colour. The roses featured on the jacket of this book are from Colombia and France and are a good example of this form of preserving – as you can see the results speak for themselves. Dried flowers have really only come into their own as an art form in the last few years. They have developed a unique style and place in the home and now sit happily alongside fresh ones. Gone are the days of dust-trap arrangements –

Dried hydrangeas vary in colour from very deep burgundy to hues of blue and turquoise.

brown, faded, muted, droopy flowers and feathers – that remained untouched and uncared for for many years.

Florists now experiment with dried flowers and have begun to treat them in a variety of new ways, arranging them differently from fresh ones. Flowers and foliage, even fruit and vegetables, are combined to create truly innovative arrangements, sculptures and one-off pieces. Today it is widely accepted that a well-conceived and executed piece can often be a striking and beautiful focal point in a living room or shop window – one that more than repays the initial cost involved. As dried-flower sculptures become more and more popular so the drying techniques have had to become much more advanced and interesting.

Choosing Flowers

✳

Although people often think that dried flowers will last for ever, they do have a shelf life. Always check the quality when you buy from a large store. Make sure that the flowers are not too dry or flaky, and that there is not too much variation in colour – they could have been in storage for a long time and be over a year old. They may even have been slightly affected by moisture from their immediate surroundings. This makes them more supple and they may seem a little fresher, but don't be deceived: as soon as they dry out they will invariably go mouldy. If in doubt, shop around: you want your arrangement to look perfect and to last for as long as possible.

Quality will vary according to where the flowers have been dried and their country of origin. Most suppliers generally buy in bulk from the same importers, but there can be a difference in quality between flowers that have been home-dried and those in a factory. Light and direct sunlight also affect them so always find out where they have been stored. Always give flowers a gentle prod as the heads sometimes look quite strong and usable when they are in bunches, but can fall apart when you come to work with them individually. Almost all flowers, particularly those of herbs such as marjoram, oregano, mint, lavender and eucalyptus, have a certain scent. The stronger the smell the fresher the flowers, but the scent will not be as strong at low temperatures as it will be in warm conditions. This is especially true of cinnamon.

When you first start to create a masterpiece you may find it difficult to decide on the number of flowers you require. This, like anything, will become easier. Either try to estimate the exact quantity and go back to the shop for more if necessary, or buy more than you need and use the extra flowers in another piece – which is what I normally do. In fact, I often end up with more flowers in the arrangement than I had intended. This can improve its appearance immensely, so, as a general rule, always use more flowers rather than less.

Once you have bought your flowers, or indeed dried your own, it is vital to store them correctly. This is often a matter of common sense. The most important rule is to keep them dry and out of direct sunlight. If possible, store them in their boxes in a darkish area. It is worth taking time to organize them into a logical storage system. This will help you avoid constantly rummaging through them which can quickly lead to battered, tired and slightly wobbly looking flowers. You could put all the herbs or fillers – flowers like achillea, linseed and marjoram – that are used to bulk out an arrangement together, or you could order them by colour. Whatever you do label them clearly and handle them carefully.

People often ask why dried flower arrangements get so dusty. They are seen as difficult to care for and impossible to keep clean and fresh looking. In reality an arrangement only becomes as dusty as the rest of a room. When it does need cleaning a hair dryer is very useful. A vacuum cleaner on low-suction power, held a few inches

Mixed arrangement.

above it, is also effective, but be careful – it might be too effective and you could lose the whole arrangement. A damp cloth is perfect for some of the glycerined flowers like eucalyptus and magnolia leaves and exotics like chilli peppers.

Foliage

✳

Contorted willow.

In the context of this book, foliage includes branches, driftwood, logs etc. as well as leaves. Contorted willow is commonly used in arrangements, along with silver birch, birch, pine, driftwood, logs, cones, lichen and moss. It is available in different cut sizes ranging from 1–8 metres / 3–25 feet. Small bunches of the wispier, curly branch-ends are also used with other flowers and foliage or on their own in urns and vases. Branches are often stripped from the tree and used as a base for a tree design or sculpture. The willow is always freshly cut and has its leaves still attached during the summer months. These must be stripped off by hand – it is advisable to wear a glove. The branch-ends go from being supple to brittle as the willow dries. It does this relatively quickly, so if you want to create a tree design that will mould in and around the ceiling in the corner of a room, do so before the wood begins to dry out in order to gain maximum effect.

Birch poles are straight sections of trunk, up to about 3 metres / 10 feet long, and are ideal for topiary

Sphagnum moss.

Stripped willow.

trees. They can also be cut down and used in other arrangements or made into containers. Driftwood, pine, logs, cones and lichen are used in different ways, either for display purposes in shop windows for example, in fireplace arrangements or at Christmas.

The two most commonly used types of moss are reindeer and flat moss. Reindeer moss is a silvery grey colour in its natural form and comes from Lapland. It is often dyed green which means it doesn't fade, it is quite spongy in appearance and texture but can be trimmed to appear flatter. Flat moss is almost like a manicured lawn, it looks more natural than reindeer moss but it fades quicker. Another very commonly used moss is sphagnum moss. Other names used to refer to this moss are: 'carpet', 'blanket', 'wet' or 'sack' moss (everyone has a different name for it). It comes in plastic sacks and is useful for filling in an arrangement and covering its base. Always make sure moss is completely dry before using it – spread it out on bin-liners and leave overnight. I once used it as a filler in a wooden box that was subsequently placed on a very expensive mahogany table; moisture worked its way through the box and the bill for the French polishers was a lot more than the cost of the original arrangement. Other types of foliage like rhododendron and eucalyptus branches are often in shop window displays, as they keep for a couple of weeks before the leaves wilt and drop off.

Panther covered in preserved magnolia leaves.

Basic Equipment

✴

Y ou can create an arrangement from flowers alone. Weave them together, as corn dollies were woven in the past, or weave dried eucalyptus stems through contorted willow branch-ends. These obviously require minimal equipment – just a pair of scissors. More ambitious projects call for some investment on your part. Some of the tools and materials listed below are essential, some just make life a lot easier.

Chicken wire – This is available in different gauges and is useful for securing around Oasis to give it added strength. It is also used for making topiary trees and for more sculptured work like wire animals (see page 84).

Drill – This is very useful for joining trunks together and making containers.

Glue gun – This is a very neat, practical way of applying glue to bind materials together. The gun heats sticks of glue to a very high temperature and then squeezes them through a nozzle. Glue guns are available from most local suppliers. Always be extremely careful when using one as the glue can burn straight through your skin.

Hammer – A standard household hammer is sufficient as long as it is sturdy enough to knock in nails.

Knife – A long kitchen knife is perfect for cutting through Oasis blocks. A small Stanley knife or something similar is also very useful.

Oasis – This water-retaining plastic foam is readily available and comes in blocks of many different shapes and sizes. Bricks are the most common. They are strong and will hold your basic arrangement securely in place. Oasis also comes in spheres which are useful for creating topiary designs.

Plaster of Paris – This is available from most local suppliers. Finishing plaster is a cheaper alternative but it takes longer to set.

Reel wire – This is a relatively thin, pliable wire on a spool. It is useful for binding bunches of flowers together, or securing moss in place around a decorative basket.

Saw – This is very useful for cutting through tough stems, branches, tree trunks and poles.

Scissors – Floral scissors are ideal as they are much stronger than ordinary household ones. If possible they should have a serrated inner edge as this makes it much easier to cut wire and also helps when cutting through tougher stems, such as those of artichokes or protea.

Staple gun – This has many uses – in particular, it simplifies securing wire netting to tree trunks. It is a lot less painful on the thumb than a hammer and nails.

Tape measure – This is essential and the one thing you can never find.

Wire – Florist's wire is now readily available and comes in different lengths and gauges. Many of the projects in this book call for a 10 mm / ½ inch gauge and 25 cm / 10 inch length. Use a heavier gauge, 15 mm to bind branches of willow together, or to attach an arrangement to a wall or a ceiling.

Advanced Equipment

✳

As you become more adventurous in your arranging and begin to advance into the realms of sculptured designs you will require more equipment. More often than not this takes the form of labour-saving electrical appliances.

Electric jigsaw – This does away with sawing by hand and is extremely useful for cutting templates and more intricate shapes and designs.

Electric sander – This is very useful for stripping down paint-covered containers, old boxes and other potential containers.

Electric screwdriver – A lazy man's tool, but once you have used it you will find it very difficult to revert to the manual method. It really is invaluable because many containers and larger tree designs need lots of screws to hold them together.

Paints – Special spray paints, available from florists, can be used on certain types of foliage and flowers – box and celosia are examples – either to change their colour or to keep it if an arrangement is going to be in direct sunlight. Their use is covered later in the book (see page 93). Other types of paints that are more widely available are gold and silver ones for spraying twigs, cones, moss, shells, etc. These are especially popular for Christmas displays.

Resin, fine mesh, fibreglass, clay etc. – Used for advanced sculptured pieces but great fun to experiment with. See chapter four.

Containers

✳

Containers are as important as the arrangements themselves and when you are planning a dried flower design it is vital to give time and thought to the relationship between the two. Together with the surroundings in which a piece will be seen, the container determines its style, colour and shape. It will also dictate its height, width and depth – balance and proportion are vital elements in a successful design. Never be nervous of experimenting. An arrangement will sometimes look striking if it is out of proportion. If it feels good to you – try it.

Containers are everywhere; it is just a case of 'seek and you shall find'. They can be made from a wide variety of materials: china, terracotta, stone, glass, wood, brass, papier mâché, lead, plastic, wire . . . almost anything. You don't have to stick to what is 'normal'. A container could be one of a dozen objects that have been lying around the house for years: old boxes, tins, porcelain, goldfish bowls or tanks. Just make sure it is in a reasonable condition and not riddled with wood-worm or rotting with damp. In fact, holders for your

Old French apple-picking or lobster baskets look good and are unusual. Making your own baskets by weaving fresh birch and willow through a wire frame is also fun and satisfying: they can be as wild as you like, and no two are the same.

arrangements can be found almost anywhere: shops, auction houses, reclamation yards, car boot sales, nurseries, attics or in your garden shed. Everyday objects like coal scuttles, iron cooking pots, biscuit tins and old wooden crates are all wonderfully versatile and can transform an arrangement. The garden is a good source of terracotta, stone, lead and maybe even marble pots and planters. Victorian terracotta pots can be found at the backs of old garden centres and, more often than not, in old potting sheds. Make sure they have no hair-line cracks which could split at a later date. And if you are putting cement in a pot, always line it with Oasis or plastic: cement expands as it dries and will crack

the containers if you don't. An ugly object can sometimes be given a face-lift with a lick of paint, woodstain or a simple scrub; and decorating or changing the colour of a dull container can transform it or make it blend into new surroundings. We often do this to cast-iron urns by adding a touch of gold with stencil paint or sanding them down and painting a marble or stone effect. Stencilling or painting designs onto a container to complement your piece can also be very effective.

With a little imagination you can make your own containers very easily: tie logs to each other for fireplace arrangements or twist twigs together to make effective baskets. Glass bowls can be filled with brightly coloured pot-pourri, soft moss, yellow sand or even broken glass. Before

Terracotta pots are probably the most popular containers. One of the main reasons is that the colour works well with most flowers. There are now huge variations in colour, shape and texture and the pots are extremely competitively priced. We invariably use old Victorian ones which were handmade and used on a vast scale before the introduction of plastic.

Lead containers are striking and can look wonderfully elegant. Older ones can be on the expensive side, but there are now good quality cast ones which are far more reasonably priced. They look particularly good with outdoor-style arrangements like box topiary or other, more formal, tree designs.

arranging the flowers put some Oasis in the middle of the bowl and fill the surrounding areas with your chosen material. If you need to use cement – for a tree design, for example – set it in a plastic bucket, put the bucket in the glass bowl and fill the bowl with moss or sand. To create your own basket for a fireplace arrangement use straight silver birch poles. First cut three or four pieces to the same length. Drill and screw these together to form the front of the basket. Cover any visible screws either by gluing small pieces of moss over them or by stripping small pieces of bark from a spare log with a sharp knife and gluing them over the screws. Then repeat the process for the sides of the basket, making sure the pieces of wood are long enough to reach the back of the fireplace. The beauty of this is that the poles can be kept very tight and smart or left slightly loose for a wilder look.

Another very simple and inexpensive way of creating a basket effect is to cover Oasis blocks with moss. Instead of putting the foam into a container, secure the blocks together with glue or wire and arrange your flowers in the normal way. Once you have finished, use 'hairpins', made by folding lengths of florist's wire, to secure moss on the Oasis. Continue adding the moss until all the blocks are covered, and you will have a wonderful, moss-effect basket.

Deciding exactly what type, colour, shape and texture of holder to use is often as inspiring as the flower arranging itself. A picture frame must be right to enhance a good painting so that it realizes its full potential, and the same is true of containers and dried flowers.

When you are in the garden or walking in woods always look for interesting branches or other items that could be used in arrangements. I once found an amazing piece of driftwood that required three people to lift it into the car while visiting friends on the coast. I ignored the usual cry that I would never find a home for it, and it is now happily ensconced in the head offices of Cartier in London with a 2.5 metre / 8 foot Panther, made out of preserved magnolia leaves, prowling along it.

Antique cast iron is very expensive but is often stunning and worth every penny. Excellent reproduction pots are now in the market, in various finishes, and as their popularity grows they should become cheaper and more widely available. They become quite rusty in colour if left outdoors and can feel very rough. Cast iron is extremely easy to paint and can completely transform an arrangement.

-2-
The Art of Design

✳

This chapter looks at designs that are based on the ground rules for arranging dried flowers. Always take your time and never rush to finish a project. Speed will come gradually with practice. Attention to detail is vital – it is what will make the piece, big or small, a success.

The Basics

✶

There are many key factors to consider when you start working on a dried flower arrangement.

The room and its surroundings play the most vital role – unless, of course, you are designing a present. It is very important to take into account its colours, textures and proportions as these will determine almost everything from the container to the size, shape, colours and textures of the final piece. One of the drawbacks with dried flowers is that when an arrangement is finished it is almost impossible to strip it down and start again without damaging some of the flowers and the Oasis.

As discussed earlier, the container also plays its part in determining the size and shape of a piece, and, to a certain degree, its colour and texture. Colour is very personal. Some people like a bright, gaudy arrangement, some are happiest with colours that are just bright or monochrome or pastel – others prefer everything to clash. Never be afraid to experiment. Don't be put off if somebody tells you that your design won't work; try it and see. Even if it doesn't, you are likely to pick up some new ideas along the way.

Movement is another very important factor when designing an arrangement. It can transform it from a two-dimensional object to a three-dimensional one and can be achieved in a number of ways depending on the piece. Wherever possible vary the heights of flowers: a marginal difference can create a totally new effect. If your arrangement calls for a variety of different flowers, vary the quantities and sizes and don't be too regimented. A popular way of creating movement is to push the ends of contorted willow or thin birch twigs through an arrangement (see page 60).

A candle with dried flowers and exotics in a cast-iron urn.

Rose Pot

＊

MATERIALS

Florist's wire	*Roses*
Knife	*Scissors*
Moss (sphagnum)	*Terracotta pot*
Oasis block (one)	

This very stylish arrangement is simple in its composition and looks stunning in almost any setting. It is also a very popular birthday or Christmas present.

It is an ideal design for anyone who has never worked with dried flowers or who has done so but wants to be more creative. It is simple to make, but achieving the perfect rose dome requires patience – or a very good eye. Don't continue if you feel your dome isn't right. Strip it down and start again – you will not be able to adjust it later. There is a huge difference between a mediocre rose pot and one that is perfect, and this project sets a precedent of patience and diligence for all later work.

Always check the quality of the roses from head to stem, making sure that the stems are not too thin and brittle and that they won't snap when you are working with them. This rose dome is set in a Victorian terracotta pot with a diameter and height of approximately 10 cm / 4 inches. You can use almost any kind of pot, but the number of roses required will increase dramatically as the diameter gets bigger.

1 *Place the Oasis block over the terracotta pot and cut it to shape using the pot as a guideline. Push the cut Oasis into the pot, and make sure it is fixed in as securely as possible. Fill in any gaps with loose bits of Oasis. Cut the florist's wire into 15 lengths of about 8 cm / 3 inches and fold them in half like hairpins; these will be used to secure the moss around the edges. Take small clumps of moss, thin them out a little and hang them over the edge of the pot. It is important to keep the moss away from the centre of the Oasis or it will interfere with the roses. Push the 'hairpins' through the moss and into the Oasis. Make sure the moss covers the rim of the pot. Continue all the way around the pot and trim off any excess with the scissors. The moss breaks up the straightness of the rose heads against the terracotta and adds movement.*

2 *Take a bunch of roses and cut the stems off about 8 cm / 3 inches below the heads. Only cut as many as you will need for the first circle of roses because the next circle will need to be slightly longer. Discard the stems or use them in other arrangements. To make stems for rose trees, cut all the stems to the same length and bind them with florist's wire at the top and bottom. Place a sphere of Oasis at one end and secure the other in a container. Cut off any excess wire.*

3 *Place the first rose into the Oasis. Put it as close to the rim of the pot as possible, at an angle of about 45°. Gauge how rough you can be with the rose, then push it as far as possible into the Oasis. Don't worry if you break some of the heads – they can always be used in other arrangements. Take the next rose and position it as close as possible to the previous one, making sure that it is at the same angle and that there is no gap between them. Continue this until you have completed a perfect circle. Try and ensure that the roses are all roughly the same size and look the same. Now make sure that all the roses are at the same angle and are not 'wavy' around the edge of the pot. If you are not happy with your circle, check it carefully as just one flower might be wrong and can easily be corrected. If there is anything amiss now, it will be even worse when the dome is finished. Always take your time: speed comes with practice.*

4 *After completing your first circle, start the second one in exactly the same way. The roses in the second circle should have slightly longer stems than those in the first circle. It is important to slightly decrease the angle at which the roses are pushed into the Oasis with each new circle and ensure that they follow a smooth, even line. Continue the circles until you are left with a small opening at the top. Fill this with a final vertical rose, or three roses if the hole is larger. When you are happy with the roses, trim off any excess moss and you are left with a beautiful rose pot.*

This technique can be applied to a number of different flowers: dahlias, echinops, poppies, chrysanthemums etc. If the stems are too fragile to push through the Oasis, insert an Oasis sphere into the rose pot to give an instant dome effect. Cut the stems off under the flower heads and then glue the heads on to the dome in the same order as above.

▶ **5** *A collection of rose pots.*

Lavender Pot

MATERIALS

Florist's wire	*Oasis block (one)*
Knife	*Scissors*
Lavender	*Terracotta pot*
Moss (reindeer)	

This arrangement of dried lavender from Provence is beautifully set off by a Victorian terracotta pot. The eye-catching symmetry of the design is due to the very level finish at the top of the lavender. Many beginners make the mistake of thinking this is done with scissors. Unfortunately, using these means you are left with a mess of stems and grey, half-cut flowers. Perfectly straight lavender can be achieved by placing small bunches in a glass or cup with the flower heads at the bottom. Shake them so that the heads align, then cut the stems to the required length and wire them together immediately to keep them level. Any bits of lavender left at the bottom of the glass or cup can be used in pot-pourri.

1 *Place the terracotta pot upside down on top of the block of Oasis. Cut the Oasis into a square shape slightly larger than the pot with the knife, then cut it so that it will fit inside the pot. The simplest way of doing this is to try and copy the shape of the pot; this gets easier with practice.*

2 *Make sure the Oasis is slightly larger than the pot and then push it firmly into it. Trim off excess Oasis so that it sits flush with the top of the pot.*

3 *Hold approximately twelve stems of perfectly straight lavender in one hand and decide what height you would like your lavender pot to be (see page 38) and cut the stem to that length.*

4 *Take a piece of florist's wire, about 25 cm / 10 inches long. Hold the twelve cut stems in your one hand and place the wire under your thumb, at right angles to the stems. Add 2¹/₂ cm / 1 inch extra for the part of the stem that will sit in the Oasis. Hold the wire approximately one-third of the way along its length with the shorter end closest to your thumb. Hold the wire in this position with your thumb and bend the long piece of wire in a straight line away from the flower heads, then wrap the short piece of wire tightly around the stems. Cut off enough wire to leave you with about 5 cm / 2 inches.*

◀ **5** *Wire about ten bunches of lavender so that they are all the same length. Place a bunch in the Oasis, about ½ cm / ¼ inch away from the edge of the pot. Push it in until it feels sturdy and straight. Start working around in a tight circle, making sure there are no gaps.*

6 *Once you get three-quarters of the way around the circle, start to place bunches in the middle of the pot, again ensuring that there are no gaps. When the middle section is full, fill in the rest of the circle. Place a piece of florist's wire around the base of the lavender bunches and tighten it. This pulls the bunches together and makes them more secure.*

7 *Cut the florist's wire into 5–8 cm / 2–3 inch lengths and fold them in half to form 'hairpins'. Take a small clump of moss, place it at the base of the lavender and secure it by pushing the hairpins through it and into the Oasis. Do this all the way around the pot and trim with scissors if necessary. For colour and variation, you could tie ribbons, raffia or rope around the base, or attach other flowers.*

Mixed Arrangement

✳

MATERIALS

Achillea 'The Pearl'	*Mercedes roses*
Blackberries	*Moss (Sphagnum)*
Chrysanthemums	*Oasis blocks*
Contorted willow (optional)	*Protea*
Florist's wire	*Scissors*
Knife	*Staples*
Larkspur	*Thin rope*
Lavender	*Wooden box*
Marjoram	

This type of arrangement offers so much scope that it is always possible to create pieces that are different. Many new ideas come from old ones, so look for fresh ways of manipulating and sculpting this kind of piece. Magazines, books, buildings, plants and – most influential of all – trees are rich sources of inspiration. Everyone knows what they would like to create; some people just find it difficult to express their concepts. Never be afraid to experiment. Be confident, and everything will come together.

1 *If your box is lidded, secure the lid in position with staples and a thin strand of rope. This arrangement is designed to sit against a wall or in a fireplace where you will not see its back; a round arrangement can be seen from all angles and might be placed on a table.*

2 *Cut the Oasis blocks so they fit securely into the box. If the box is deeper than the Oasis put a layer of moss on the bottom (make sure it is totally dry), then place the Oasis on top of it.*

3 *Wire the individual flowers into the bunch sizes required. This will vary with the different types of flower, size of container and personal preference. This arrangement uses mercedes roses in bunches of threes and fives, protea in single stems and blackberries in bunches of threes and fives — always work in odd numbers rather than even ones as this gives a better overall shape. These are the 'static' flowers in the arrangement. The chrysanthemums, larkspur, achillea, marjoram and lavender add movement and are wired to suit individual tastes.*

4 *Start by placing the first flower – in this case the chrysanthemums – in the centre at the back. To ensure you get the correct height, always cut flowers slightly longer than necessary, remember that about an inch will go into the Oasis. It is far easier to keep on cutting them down rather than to extend them. If you do cut them too short, or if the stems themselves are too short, wire an extension on to the existing stem. Use another cut stem that is strong enough – a rose stem or even a piece of thin, straight willow.*

5 *Continue adding bunches of flowers, working left and then right from the original flower. Here the tallest flower sits in the middle of the box. The other flowers are angled down towards the bottom corners of the container to create a graceful curve.*

6 *Work your way down in a line towards the front of the box. Be careful not to come down too steeply or your arrangement will look flat; it is important to keep a good angle. Experiment as you go, and remember that once you are happy and confident you can adapt these rules to suit your tastes.*

7 *You now have two quarters to fill in. Position the flowers in whatever way you feel looks best. It is easier to work with a variety of flowers rather than with three different types, for example, as you are less likely to end up with lots of patches of the same colour. Once you have filled in the two sides check that they are equally balanced. You can do a little tweaking when the arrangement is finished, pulling out the flowers a little and filling in small gaps.*

8 *Contorted willow would give this type of arrangement a certain wild quality. Cut the ends of the willow branches to about 15–20 cm / 6–8 inches, wrap some florist's wire around the bottom of the stems and then poke the stems into the arrangement. Insert about twelve pieces. To do this type of arrangement in a round container, position the tallest flower in the middle of the piece to obtain the height you require. Work away from this centre flower, first in a line to its left and then in a line to its right, ensuring that the two sides are symmetrical. Then turn the arrangement around and work down the two remaining sides at right angles to these first lines of flowers so that you are left with four quarters. Fill in each quarter.*

Wheat in Terracotta Planter

✳

MATERIALS

Florist's wire	*Scissors*
Knife	*Terracotta pots (two)*
Moss (sphagnum)	*Thin rope*
Oasis blocks	*Wheat*
Oblong wooden box	

To create this very simple, striking arrangement, follow the instructions for the Lavender Pot (see page 38). This particular design is for a large fireplace, but would look just as good on a shelf or in an alcove. Wheat keeps its rigidity when it is harvested at quite an early stage, so it is best to buy it when it is still slightly green. After a short period it will become a lovely golden colour. Leave it in sunlight to speed up this process. One huge advantage of using wheat is that it won't lose its colour, and will therefore last for years and years.

Place two terracotta pots inside an oblong wooden box and secure them into place by filling the gaps with the sphagnum moss. Then, following the instructions for the Lavender Pot, fill them with wired lavender stems. Put rope around the stems to finish off the piece. The same effect can be gained using rose pots. Wheat looks great, as do moss trees. Try using three pots, perhaps with wheat in the centre and lavender on either side of it. Four pots can also look good. Keep experimenting.

▶ *Another alternative is to add lavender around the base of the wheat to give a delightful contrast in colour and texture.*

Topiary Rose Tree

MATERIALS

Birch pole	*Plaster of Paris or quick-drying cement*
Glue for securing the Oasis ball	*Roses (4–5 bunches)*
Glue gun and glue sticks	*Saw*
Knife	*Scissors*
Moss (flat)	*Terracotta or similar pot*
Oasis (one ball, one block)	

Topiary spheres are popular designs that are stunning in their simplicity. This rose tree is relatively simple to make. A perfect arrangement – a completely symmetrical sphere with all the roses the same size – takes time and patience. It is all too easy to rush a piece like this, thinking it is easy, and end up with an oddly shaped, uneven sphere. Take your time: speed will come with practice.

1 *Saw the stem pole to the height you want your tree to be; here it is approximately 20 cm / 8 inches. Cut small thin strips from the Oasis block and place them around the base and sides of the pot, fill the pot with plaster of Paris or cement. The Oasis will prevent the pot cracking when the filling dries and expands. Place the branch in the plaster or cement and then wait for the filling to set. Secure the Oasis ball on the top of the branch with a dollop of glue and then push the branch in about 4 cm / 1¹/₂ inches. Cover the base by gluing moss on to the filling with the glue gun.*

2 *Cut the roses about 5 cm / 2 inches from the base of their heads. Place the first rose at the very top of the Oasis ball. Push the stem all the way in until the rose head touches the Oasis. If it does not feel secure add a little glue. Place the next rose against this one ensuring that there is no gap. Don't worry about breaking the stems if they are fragile. They can either be glued into place or used in other arrangements.*

▶ **3** *Continue working your way around the Oasis ball, from top to bottom, until you have made a full circle of roses.*

4 *Make another circle of roses, this time around the centre of the Oasis ball. This will leave you with four equal quarters.*

5 *Fill in the quarters by packing the roses tightly together. Your tree will be a perfect sphere of roses if you follow this method, rather than something that vaguely resembles a ball.*

6 *The finished tree. Although the little green leaves that are normally attached to roses look very attractive on the sphere, they will eventually go brown. You can always pull them out when this happens, but it is often a good idea to remove them beforehand, especially if it is to be a gift.*

Protea

MATERIALS

Chicken wire (medium gauge)	*Moss (sphagnum)*
Contorted willow	*Protea*
Florist's wire	*Scissors (serrated), or small hand saw*

The protea is the national flower of South Africa and comes in its natural form – a very soft pink – or, dyed a wonderful flame-orange and red, as shown here. These ones opposite have been dried and preserved in an antique Indian container. Branch-ends of contorted willow give the composition movement and an attractively wild quality. Each piece of willow was wired and then slotted into the arrangement. This arrangement is in a hallway where it looks colourful and dramatic.

1 *Cut enough chicken wire to create a dome effect and also to reach the bottom of the container so that the arrangement can be secured in place. Leave a hole in the bottom of the wire – you will have to fill the container and dome with moss.*

2 *Fill the chicken wire with moss. Press it down firmly into the container to hold it in place. Keep the moss inside the dome looser, as you have to pass the protea stems and wire through it. Use serrated scissors or a small hand saw to cut the protea stems about 8–10 cm / 3–4 inches from the base of the flowers. Wire the individual stems with florist's wire, keeping the wire as long as possible.*

3 *Start at the rim of the container and pass a wired protea through the chicken wire until the base of the protea is on the rim of the container. Wrap the end of the wire around the chicken wire to hold the protea in place. Place the second protea next to the first one. Make sure they are exactly level at the top. Continue this process until you have completed a full circle.*

4 *Now create a second circle as close as possible to the first one.*

5 *Continue building ever-decreasing circles, angling the protea slightly more each time until you can place one final protea vertically in the middle of the arrangement.*

▶ **6** *If the dome is not totally symmetrical you should be able to manipulate the offending protea into shape. Use a little moss to cover up the gaps where you can see chicken wire. Add the contorted willow.*

Different Arrangements Using Protea

Protea are exotic rather than dried flowers. They are very tough in texture and are wonderful for spicing up softer dried arrangements. When they come to us their stems are about 20–25 cm / 8–10 inches long and as tough as wood. You can break them off with your hands but they are unpredictable and will break off right under the flower head if you are not careful, leaving you with nothing to attach the wire to. This is why it is advisable to use a pair of serrated scissors or a small hand saw.

If you are making a complete sphere of protea, on a pole of silver birch, for example, you can use an Oasis ball as the base rather than chicken wire and moss. Remember, though, that protea heads are large – you may well have to use smaller ones than you originally intended or they will stick out too far. Always cover the

The sizes of the spheres are varied and attached to contorted willow trunks in this visually dramatic arrangement. To add movement and create a much wilder design insert contorted willow through the spheres.

Oasis ball with chicken wire as the Oasis may crack and break when a lot of stems are pushed into it. This is important as this always happens when you put the last few stems in – never when you start. The wire will keep everything intact and hold the Oasis if it cracks. Attach the wire to the pole with heavy-duty staples or a hammer and nails.

Protea look striking in festive garlands and swags, and especially on Christmas trees – attach them to the ends of branches as an alternative to candles. They are also very good for making pot-pourri as they look beautiful mixed in with dried mushrooms and fruit slices, pine cones and cinnamon. Buy pot-pourri essence, mix all the ingredients in a bin-bag and add the essence. Tie the bag up and leave it for a few days – you will have the most original pot-pourri around.

The protea in the arrangements shown here have been dyed, so the colour will last for a very long time.

The spikes on the protea heads have been cut off – they are almost like needles – and glued into an Oasis sphere which is set in a small, cast-iron urn. The glue is necessary to hold the spikes to the Oasis as they are too short to be inserted deeply into the sphere. Arrange them in circles and glue moss around the base of each one to conceal the Oasis.

This arrangement on the left is also shown as part of a window display above.

−3−

Floral Sculptures

✳

The more advanced arrangements in this chapter have a sculptural feel and range from spiral topiary trees to wire-framed animals. They make use of many of the techniques described in Chapter Two.

Topiary Spiral
Moss Tree

✳

MATERIALS

Birch pole	*Plaster of Paris*
Chicken wire (medium gauge)	*Moss (flat)*
Container	*Saw*
Florist's wire	*Scissors*
Glue gun & glue sticks (optional)	*Staple gun or hammer and nails*
Oasis (block)	

Spirals are fantastic shapes to work with as they convey height without being too heavy. They range from tiny to very large and can be created with a number of different materials, from the moss shown here, to magnolia leaves, celosia, lavender, sea shells, round pebbles and many more. The shape of a spiral can be altered in several ways: the gaps in the loops can be varied, for example you can stretch or compact the spiral, or the lower half of the tree can be made much thicker than the top half to change the perspective.

1 *Saw the birch pole to your desired height and secure it in the pot with the plaster of Paris (see page 56, step 1). Cut the chicken wire into a length that will be long enough to wrap around the pole. Make a 'sausage roll' of the chicken wire and sphagnum moss. Start it off thinly at one end and make it gradually fatter at the other. Wrap this up fairly tightly and secure the ends and seam by cutting the edges of the wire and twisting them together.*

2 *Wrap the chicken wire filled with moss around the pole into the spiral shape you require. Secure the base on the pole with a staple gun or hammer and nails. Continue securing it to the pole as you go up.*

▶ **3** *Attach the end of the chicken wire to the pole. Suit the final length to your own design by tapering the wire to a point and varying the angle.*

4 *Now you are ready to add the flat moss to the frame. There are two ways of doing this. One is to use glue but this can result in burnt fingers and is more costly, especially if you are making a large tree. The simplest method is to cut the florist's wire into small lengths and bend them into 'hairpins'. Place a piece of moss against the spiral and secure it with hairpins. Press them into the moss as far as possible and make sure you use enough hairpins to keep it secure. Continue doing this until the wire is covered. When joining the moss pieces together, don't use scissors to smooth the edges. Keep them rough and pick away any brown or earthy bits with your fingers. You will achieve a much smoother join that is not easily visible.*

▶ **5** *The overall look should be as smooth and natural as possible.*

Mirror Frame

✳

MATERIALS

Birch poles	*Saw*
Church candles	*Screwdriver*
Drill	*Screws*
Glue gun and glue sticks	*Tape measure*
Adhesive silicon	*Terracotta pots (two)*
Moss	*Wood planks*
Plain mirror	

Mirrors transform a room, hallway or bathroom – and can be objects of beauty in themselves. Plain wooden frames are no longer enough. The popularity of metalwork, which has introduced a sense of movement in the design of everyday furniture, has inspired some quite spectacular mirrors: mirrors surrounded by contorted willow trees growing out of a eucalyptus frame with chillies and protea; and mirror frames made out of driftwood and shells, etc. This mirror is very simple in its finished design, but shows how to make a base for a decorative frame. Once you have mastered this you will be able to evolve your own ideas.

1 *First secure the mirror on a frame that can be used as a base for the decorations. To do this, cut planks of wood so that they overlap the back of the mirror by approximately 4 cm / 1¹/₂ inches all the way around. Secure the wood to the mirror with adhesive silicon (available from local suppliers). Just put blobs of the adhesive around the outside edge of the mirror and apply the wood. Don't worry about the corners as these will be covered up by the frame. Wait until the glue has set and the wood is firmly attached to the mirror.*

2 *Measure the sides of the mirror and saw two pieces of birch pole to the required length. Drill holes through the frame about a quarter of the way from the top and the bottom, on one side. Hold one of the birch pieces on the edge of the mirror surface, then screw through the frame and into the pole. Make sure it is secure. Do this on the second side. Saw two more poles for the top and bottom of the mirror. They must slot into the gap between the two side poles. Saw them individually – they are sure to be different lengths – then drill and secure them in position.*

3 *You should now have a single birch frame surrounding your mirror. Repeat the process, but make the poles slightly longer. Drill each one and use screws to attach it to the pole below at a 45° angle. The screws will be covered later with moss. Now repeat the process to make a third frame and attach it to the second one. Make sure once again that it is secure. Glue pieces of moss between the edge of the mirror and the first birch frame, then between the other frames. Use a glue gun for this. Finally, cover any screws that are showing with moss.*

4 *Place two candles in each of two terracotta pots; make sure they are firmly fixed and stable by surrounding them with moss. Screw the pots into the bottom of the mirror. Handle the mirror very carefully. Always have somebody at hand to help you move it, and always work on a very even surface – you don't want to get seven years of bad dried flower arranging under your belt! Make sure you have strong fittings for hanging the mirror as it will probably be heavy.*

▶ **5** *The finished mirror*

82

Wire-Framed Frog

✳

MATERIALS

Chicken wire	*Moss (reindeer and sphagnum)*
Florist's wire	*Pliers (optional)*
Glue gun and glue sticks	*Scissors*

Wire-framed animals are becoming increasingly popular and range from teddy bears to more elaborate creatures. Over the years we have been commissioned to make some wonderful pieces. They include a life-size panther (see page 109), and elephants and bears made from reindeer moss; forty-two 1 metre / 3 foot high footballers and supporters for Euro '96 created with preserved rose petals and leaves (see page 116–19); a flying Pegasus with a 4 metre / 14 foot wingspan that used white dahlia heads; and, more recently, a full-size donkey made out of copper tubing that will actually have fresh yew growing up and through it. These animals are great fun to make and experiment with and are unusual presents. Always begin with one that is simple to design – a cat, dog or frog – then when you have become accustomed to using chicken wire and have mastered the basics you can be more adventurous. A stronger frame than chicken wire will be needed for larger sculptures as the wire will not support their weight. The panther, for example, has a wooden base. Children's books are inspirational when you are looking for shapes and sizes. Make scale drawings of larger animals to work out the exact proportions, even with the smaller frames it is helpful to sketch or trace the design on a sheet of paper for reference.

1 Take a strip of chicken wire and cut it to approximately twice the size of the base of the frog, here it is approximately 70 cm / 28 inches. Bend the chicken wire upwards to make the lower half of the main body and shape it to look like a frog's torso. For a realistic shape, add small bits of chicken wire to create the necessary lumps and bumps; now make the main body – it musn't be too tubular. Join the wire together by cutting along the edges and bending the cut wires over the main chicken wire. You may need to borrow a strong pair of hands – or use a pair of pliers. Leave an opening at one end and put the sphagnum moss inside once this section of the frame is ready. Make sure the moss is not too tight: you will have to pin wires through it. Once you are happy with the shape, seal up the end as described above. You now have a solid body.

2 The limbs can be attached either before or after the main body is finished. I tend to add them before. It is easier to secure them tightly on the frame and make sure they will not fall off. Now add the other features: eyes, ears and mouth. These are secured as described in step 1, but make sure that they are very firmly attached. You now have a naked wire-framed frog. If you are not happy with it you can always add more wire and moss, or cut off pieces to change the shape.

3 *Use glue or florist's wire to cover the whole frame with reindeer moss. If you are using wire, cut into 15 cm / 6 inch lengths and fold them in half to make 'hairpins'. Make sure the hairpins are tightly folded as they must not be visible when they are in place holding the moss. It is advisable to use the glue gun for more intricate areas like eyes as it is difficult to secure the moss without the hairpins showing. Finer details like blackberries for eyes and straight willow for whiskers and hair can be added later.*

Box Topiary Trees

✳

MATERIALS

Bin-liner	Moss (reindeer)
Birch pole	Moss-green florist's spray paint
Box	Oasis (bricks and two different-
Chicken wire	sized spheres)
Container	Plaster of Paris
Contorted willow (optional)	Saw
Florist's wire	Scissors
Garden shears	Staple gun, or hammer and nails
Knife	

Box is very popular for topiary or outdoor sculptures and is trimmed and trained into a huge variety of shapes. It is now grown commercially in planters and cut specifically into spirals and spheres as well as animals. However, this kind of topiary is expensive and needs a great deal of looking after. It is also very difficult to keep the box alive indoors, particularly in dark corners and hallways. We use fresh box bought in bundles, cut from hedgerows, this is one of the only forms of fresh box that we use.

1 *Cut the Oasis bricks into strips. Line the container with the bin-liner and then the Oasis to prevent any cracking as the plaster of Paris expands. Saw the birch pole to the height you require and then pour the plaster of Paris into the container. Remember that the plaster will set very fast, so make sure you have everything ready.*

2 *Place the pole in the centre of the plaster. Make sure it is far enough in and that it is completely central and straight. Hold the pole until the plaster has set. Now place the larger Oasis sphere on top of the pole and push down a little so that the foam is indented. Use a knife to cut a hole through the Oasis, using the indentation as a guideline. Be careful not to make the hole too wide — always cut it a little thinner for a better fit. Push the sphere down to the position you require; remember to leave space for the box. Repeat the process with the smaller sphere.*

3 *Cut a piece of chicken wire large enough to surround the larger Oasis sphere, and attach it to the pole above and below the Oasis. Use a staple gun or hammer and nails, and make sure the wire is very secure. Cut the box into small bundles of approximately six to eight sprigs, discarding any woody bits, and make them into bunches with florist's wire.*

4 *Insert the box in the Oasis following the method used for the Topiary Rose Tree on page 54. Trim the ends of the box with scissors or the garden shears to give it a smooth elegant edge. This becomes much easier with practice. Repeat steps 3 and 4 with the smaller sphere.*

5 *Once you have completed both spheres and are happy with the results, spray the box with green spray paint; without this it will gradually go brown and shrivel. Leave the tree for about a week to allow the leaves to dry out completely and then give it a final spray. Place the moss at the top of the urns and twine contorted-willow branches around the birch poles if you want to add more movement (see page 88).*

Celosia Tree

MATERIALS

Chicken wire	Saw
Celosia	Scissors
Drill	Screws and screwdriver
Florist's Wire	Staple gun
Glue gun and glue sticks	Terracotta pot
Moss (flat and reindeer)	Vine or wood
Plaster of Paris	

Celosia is red with a wonderful, velvety texture. Its stems are quite long and it works well in mixed dried flower arrangements where it adds a touch of brightness. However, I think it is at its best when used on its own, as here. This design is very similar to a bonsai tree, but it can look equally fantastic when it stands over 1.8 metres / 6 feet high.

1 *Join your vine or wood together if necessary, using a drill and screws. We used two pieces of Spanish grape vine. Remember to cover up the screw-holes with cut pieces of bark; using a glue gun for this.*

2 *Use Plaster of Paris to set the vine or wood in the terracotta pot (see page 56). Decide where you would like to place the clumps of celosia – you will probably change your mind once you start. It is a good idea to make one clump and then make a final decision.*

◀ **3** *Cut some chicken wire to roughly the required size of the clump. Staple it on to the vine or wood and then manipulate it to the basic shape you want.*

▶ **4** *Continue manipulating the chicken wire until it is the shape you require. Leave an opening and stuff it with moss. Secure it when you are happy with the shape and its position on the vine or wood. You can tweak it further or add extensions if you still want to change the shape.*

5 *Once you have finished one of the 'clumps', it can be manipulated to create an undulating shape which will give the arrangement its movement. Try not to make these 'clumps' flat – if you do, the design will have no depth.*

6 *Cut the celosia heads off at the base of the flowers and glue them on to the chicken wire, starting where you like. Work with small pieces of celosia – they will adhere more securely to the chicken wire. In this arrangement only the top half of the 'clump' is covered with celosia. The underside is covered with flat moss as the contrast works well and also adds to the movement. Allow the celosia to go 'up and down' where it hits the moss. It should not end in a straight line.*

7 *Make sure that all the wire is tightly covered in celosia and that there are no gaps. If there are a few then you can glue more celosia over them, as this arrangement benefits from being uneven. Add reindeer moss under the clumps of celosia. The colours and textures complement each other and give contrast and more movement to the design. Attach the moss with florist's wire bent into 'hairpins', or use a glue gun – but remember to watch your hands.*

Additional Ideas

✳

Here are some further examples of pieces that you can create using the techniques you have learnt in the previous chapters.

▶ *Two small spheres of glued chrysanthemums on straight willow were cemented into Victorian terracotta pots painted with floral designs. They are relatively inexpensive to make and look great sitting either side of a mantelpiece.*

◀ *Preserved reindeer moss was pinned on to different-sized Oasis spheres attached to a wonderful piece of Spanish grape vine that had been cemented into a wooden container. We found the piece of wood first, cemented it into place and then decided on the size of the spheres and where to place them.*

▶ *This fireplace arrangement is striking in its simplicity, and shows how well tree designs can work in different settings. Preserved baby green eucalyptus was cut and wired into lengths of about 20–25 cm / 8–10 inches, pushed into a sphere of Oasis and chicken wire, placed on contorted willow branches and cemented into an old Indian grain measure.*

◀ A sphere of Oasis and chicken wire was placed on two pieces of aged, contorted willow and covered with marjoram, which has a wonderful, long-lasting aroma. The wood gives the arrangement a sense of movement that contrasts with the static marjoram sphere.

◀ Varying the flowers, sizes and containers used in the same basic design creates different effects. This arrangement would sit quite happily with fresh flowers in a room as it is a very sculptured piece of work. It uses chrysanthemums to create an unusual sculptured tree.

▶ Three moss trees on contorted willow were cemented into a wooden trough at different heights.

◀ A piece of Spanish grape vine was cemented into a large Victorian pot. Two different-sized Oasis spheres are held together with chicken wire as the lavender is likely to split them. The lavender was cut into approximately 12 cm / 5 inch lengths. It was wired in the usual manner and then secured in the Oasis, using the quarter method (described in the Rose Tree Topiary on page 54), to achieve perfect spheres. The only slight drawback with this arrangement is that the lavender is delicate, so needs to be positioned where it will not be knocked or moved too often.

◀ Three moss spheres were placed
on a straight birch pole and secured
with glue. The pole was then
cemented into this unusual terracotta
container.

▶ These striking yellow spheres are
made out of hundreds of
chrysanthemum heads, individually
glued on to Oasis spheres. This was a
long and laborious task, but the
results speak for themselves. The
spheres were placed on five birch poles
which were cemented into painted
wooden pots.

-4-
Creating a Masterpiece

✳

The designs and sculptures in this chapter don't follow the usual forms of construction and will, I hope, inspire you to create your own, truly individual, pieces. There are no real set rules or ways of working. It is important to experiment and if you don't succeed at first, then try again until you are happy with the result. This panther was made from dark green magnolia leaves which have an almost leathery feel, and a slight sheen that comes from the glycerine used in the preserving process. A wooden frame provided the backbone, head and legs. The main shape was built up with chicken wire and fine mesh which was covered with a thin layer of papier mâché. The magnolia leaves were glued to this.

HARLEQUIN & BALLERINA

These sculptures, a ballerina on the right and a harlequin on the left, are about 2 metres / 7 feet high which gives them an incredible presence and feeling of movement. They are remarkable because they are balancing – the harlequin on one foot and the ballerina on her toes – yet remain totally stable. Each figure was made up on a wooden pole frame that provided its backbone and structure. A small-gauge chicken-wire frame was attached to this to give the body shape and achieve the balance.

The frame was then secured to a wooden block with a steel rod through the leg which gave it the necessary strength. The finished shape was covered with a very fine skin of tissue paper and the leaves, flowers, etc. were glued to this with wood glue. It is useful to create a number of colour drawings to scale in order to work out in advance where these will go and what flowers and textures to use.

For the harlequin we used: eucalyptus leaves for his skin, skeleton leaves for his collar ruff, oak leaves for his fiddle, apple slices on his jacket, orange slices as buckles on his shoes, and celosia, achillea, curry flowers, dahlia heads, bulrushes, straight willow and raffia everywhere else.

For the ballerina we used: magnolia leaves on her legs, preserved rose petals on her shoes, dahlia heads and bulrushes on her body, apple slices on her arms, skeleton leaves for her hat, eucalyptus for her skin and yellow batao as the studs on her legs.

PRESERVED ROSES & SHOES

This glass bowl was filled with Oasis blocks with a layer of flat moss placed between the Oasis and the glass. If you have difficulty holding the Oasis in place, carefully put a couple of strips of thin florist's tape across its top and attach the tape to the edges of the glass bowl. It will be covered up by the flowers. The white roses are the preserved ones shown on the front cover of the book, and because of the way they are preserved they really are a true, pure white. This piece shows how just one type of flower in one colour, arranged in a simple design, can be a masterpiece.

▶ *The shoes are about 12 cm / 5 inches high so can sit quite happily on a mantelpiece or in a display cabinet. They are on a wire-mesh frame and the flowers – achillea 'The Pearl' – were glued in place. They were cut very carefully from their stems, as evenly, and as close to the bud, as possible. The flowers must all be of a similar size to create a balanced finish.*

CONTORTED WILLOW & DAFFODIL

The main body for this tree design was made from contorted willow and then set in a large Victorian pot. The spirals around the branches are green leaves (actually made from silk). Clumps of about ten were wired around the stems so that they splayed open and give a slightly spiky effect. Protea heads look as though they are growing out of the leaves. The tree is extraordinarily lifelike – it is difficult to tell that it is not still growing and flowering – and I know for a fact that one person watered it when she first saw it.

▶ *This 6 foot / 1.8 metre daffodil was constructed for a spring window display, and since creating it we have made a number of other tall flowers, including a set of Scottish thistles. The main stem – a trunk of contorted willow – was covered in magnolia leaves. The rest of the frame was made with chicken wire and covered in yellow tissue paper. Yellow dahlia heads were glued all over the front of the daffodil leaving the yellow tissue paper showing at the back. The edges of the flower were made from yellow chrysanthemums and the centre stamens with straight willow stems. The ends of these are covered in dahlia heads.*

FOOTBALL PLAYERS

The footballers here and overleaf were created for the Euro '96 final. The Grosvenor House Hotel ballroom was transformed into a football stadium for an evening and these figures, rather than fresh flowers, were the centre-table arrangement. Twenty-two players stood in the middle of the ballroom, on tables marked out with Astro turf and goal posts, and twenty-one other figures including substitutes, spectators, corner posts, referee and linesmen, were positioned around them.

Because of the scale and detail required, each player was only about 75 cm / 2¹/₂ feet tall. We made a clay model of a footballer from which we took resin moulds for the arms, legs, body and head. We then pressed very fine mesh into them to create the frames for the body parts and ended up with eighty-six legs, eighty-six arms and forty-three heads and bodies. These were joined together into various poses and strengthened with fibreglass resin. There was no need for a skin to glue the flowers to as they were attached directly to the mesh.

We used preserved rose petals for the footballers' strips as they have a lovely strong, velvety texture and, given the scale we were working to, were fairly flexible. As the petals come in red, yellow, white and peach, other colours had to be applied to the figures with florist's spray paint. Green preserved eucalyptus leaves were used for the figures' skin and black eucalyptus leaves for boots.

To finish, each figure was mounted on a metal stand to add movement. The end result was stunning, if a little surreal.

Acknowledgments

I would like to thank all my family for their love and support especially my sister Kerry for making it happen in the beginning. Beth Vaughan and Susan Haynes for their help and understanding. Phil Starling for his amazing photography. Miggy Liversidge, Jenny Goss, Daniel Slack, Peter and Kay Robson, David Ellinor, and to all our clients and friends who have all helped make this book possible.